defending the
military
marriage

homebuilders
COUPLES SERIES®

defending the
military
marriage

jim fishback
lt. col. us army (ret.) &
bea fishback

FAMILYLIFE®

Little Rock, Arkansas

DEFENDING THE MILITARY MARRIAGE
FamilyLife Publishing®
5800 Ranch Drive
Little Rock, Arkansas 72223
1-800-FL-TODAY • FamilyLife.com

FLTI, d/b/a FamilyLife®, is a ministry of Campus Crusade for Christ International®.

Military Ministry is a ministry of Campus Crusade for Christ International®.

ISBN: 978-1-60200-642-3

Military Ministry
PO Box 120124
Newport News, VA 23612-0124
1-800-444-6006
MilitaryMinistry.org
info@MilitaryMinistry.org

Design: Brand Navigation, LLC
Cover image: © iStockphoto.com/inhauscreative

Printed in the United States of America
17 16 15 14 13   1 2 3 4 5

FAMILYLIFE

Unless the LORD builds the house,
those who build it labor in vain.

PSALM 127:1

The HomeBuilders Couples Series®

Building Your Marriage to Last
Improving Communication in Your Marriage
Resolving Conflict in Your Marriage
Mastering Money in Your Marriage
Building Teamwork in Your Marriage
Growing Together in Christ
Building Up Your Spouse
Managing Pressure in Your Marriage
Defending the Military Marriage
Making Your Marriage Deployment Ready

The HomeBuilders Parenting Series®

Improving Your Parenting
Establishing Effective Discipline for Your Children
Guiding Your Teenagers
Raising Children of Faith
Defending the Military Family

Marriage should be enjoyed, not endured. It is meant to be a vibrant relationship between two people who love each other with passion, commitment, understanding, and grace. So secure is the bond God desires between a husband and a wife that He uses it to illustrate the magnitude of Christ's love for the church (see Ephesians 5:25–33).

Do you have that kind of love in your marriage?

Relationships often fade over time as people drift apart—but only if the relationship is left unattended. We have a choice in the matter; our marriages don't have to grow dull. Perhaps we just need to give them some attention.

That's the purpose behind the HomeBuilders Couples Series®—to provide you a way to give your marriage the attention it needs and deserves. This is a biblically based small-group study because, in the Bible, God has given the blueprint for building a loving and secure marriage. His plan is designed to enable a man and a woman to grow together in a mutually satisfying relationship and then to reach out to others with the love of Christ. Ignoring God's plan may lead to isolation and, in far too many cases, the breakup of the home.

Whether your marriage needs a complete makeover or just a few small adjustments, we encourage you to consult God's design. Although written several thousand years ago, Scripture still speaks clearly and powerfully about the conflicts and challenges men and women face.

Do we really need to be part of a group? Couldn't we just go through this study as a couple?

While you could work through the study as a couple, you would miss the opportunity to connect with friends and to learn from one another's experiences. You will find that the questions in each session not only help you grow closer to your spouse, but they also create an environment of warmth and fellowship with other couples as you study together.

What does it take to lead a HomeBuilders group?

Leading a group is much easier than you may think, because the leader is simply a facilitator who guides the participants through the discussion questions. You are not teaching the material but are helping the couples discover and apply biblical truths. The special dynamic of a HomeBuilders group is that couples teach themselves.

The study guide you're holding has all the information and guidance you need to participate in or lead a HomeBuilders group. You'll find leader's notes in the back of the guide, and additional helps are posted online at FamilyLife.com/Resources.

What is the typical schedule?

Most studies in the HomeBuilders Couples Series are six to eight weeks long, indicated by the number of sessions in the guide. The sessions are designed to take sixty minutes in the group with a project for the couples to complete between sessions.

Isn't it risky to talk about your marriage in a group?

The group setting should be enjoyable and informative—and non-threatening. THREE SIMPLE GROUND RULES will help ensure that everyone feels comfortable and gets the most out of the experience:

1. Share nothing that will embarrass your spouse.
2. You may pass on any question you do not want to answer.
3. If possible, as a couple complete the HomeBuilders project between group sessions.

What other help does FamilyLife offer?

Our list of marriage and family resources continues to grow. Visit FamilyLife.com to learn more about our

- Weekend to Remember® and other live conferences and events;
- slate of radio broadcasts, including the nationally syndicated *FamilyLife Today*®, *Real FamilyLife with Dennis Rainey*®, and *FamilyLife This Week*®;
- Military Art of Marriage® event (visit TheArtof MarriageOps.com for details);
- interactive products for parents, couples, small-group leaders, and one-to-one mentors; and
- an assortment of blogs, forums, and other online connections.

Lt. Col. Jim Fishback, USA (ret.), is a graduate of the United States Military Academy at West Point and served with the United States Army for more than twenty years. After retiring, the Fishbacks joined the staff of Cru and are currently working in a partnership with the Military Ministry and FamilyLife. Jim and Bea live in the United Kingdom, bringing the resources of these ministries to military personnel stationed in Europe and the Middle East. They have two grown children, Jamie and Joni.

contents

Dear Military Couples,

When we are married, we make a commitment to "love, honor, and cherish" each other for the rest of our lives. But it usually doesn't take long to discover that building a lasting marriage is a more demanding assignment than we realized it would be.

This is especially true for couples in the military. You face unique challenges that can put tremendous pressure on your love, teamwork, and commitment. *Defending the Military Marriage* takes time-tested principles that have helped millions of couples and applies them to the military lifestyle. You will find this study practical, refreshing, and easy to use.

Psalm 127:1 says, "Unless the LORD builds the house, those who build it labor in vain." This study, part of the HomeBuilders Couples Series, will help you apply biblical truths to your marriage. You will learn them in an encouraging environment along with other couples who face the same pressures in their relationships.

This is a life-changing tool that will help you build the type of marriage you've always wanted. We hope that this small-group experience will be one of the best experiences of your lives.

Yours for stronger military families,

—Dennis Rainey
    President, FamilyLife
—Jeff Oster
    Lieutenant General, US Marine Corps (ret.)
    Executive Director, Military Ministry

acknowledgments

We want to acknowledge Bea's father, Job Doty, who served for five years and was injured three times during World War II; and Jim's father, Col. Jesse Fishback, USA (ret.), who served in the Army for over thirty years and fought in three wars.

Thanks to our children, Jamie and Joni, who moved many times and lived in three countries during our time in the military.

Thanks to our colaborers in FamilyLife and the Military Ministry and to our team around the world. We would not be here without you.

Finally, we want to thank the men and women of our armed forces and their families who sacrifice so much so that we might continue to enjoy our freedom. Not since the Revolutionary War have so few borne the burdens of so many. We pray the truths contained in this book will encourage and equip you as you continue to defend our constitution and way of life.

—Jim and Bea Fishback

1

Basic
Training

Learn basic principles that will refresh your perspective on your marriage mission.

warm-up

1. Introduce yourself to the group. Then, taking no more than two minutes, you or your spouse tell the group how the two of you met.
2. Tell the group how many years you have served in the military, and how many different assignments you've had.
3. If you could have a dream assignment, where would it be and why?

blueprints

Military and Marriage

Every marriage relationship is affected by many factors—the family backgrounds of the husband and the wife, the choices each has made through the years, their friends, their places of employment, and so on. As part of the military, you've learned by now that your lifestyle affects your marriage in many unique ways.

1. Describe the positive influences the military lifestyle can have on a marriage and family.

2. Describe some of the pressures the military lifestyle puts on a marriage.

Marriage Training Principles

To make a marriage work in the military environment, a couple needs some basic training for building a solid relationship. To understand these basics, we are going to turn to what we could call *God's Field Manual for Living,* the Bible.

Let's begin by reading from the creation account in the book of Genesis. After creating man, God determined that something was missing:

> Then the Lord God said, "It is not good that the man should be alone; I will make him a helper fit for him." So out of the ground the Lord God formed every beast of the field and every bird of the heavens and brought them to the man to see what he would call them. And whatever the man called every living creature, that was its name. The man gave names to all livestock and to the birds of the heavens and to every beast of the field. But for Adam there was not found a helper fit for him. So the Lord God caused a deep sleep to fall upon the man, and while he slept took one of his ribs and closed up its place with flesh. And the rib that the Lord God had taken from the man he made into a woman and brought her to the man. Then the man said, "This at last is bone of my bones and flesh of my flesh; she shall be called Woman, because she was taken out of Man."
>
> Therefore a man shall leave his father and his mother and hold fast to his wife, and they shall become one flesh. And the man and his wife were both naked and were not ashamed. (Genesis 2:18–25)

Training Principle #1:
Make Your Marriage Your Priority

3. In this passage, God says a husband and wife should "leave" their parents and "cleave" ("hold fast") to their spouse. What do you think it means to "leave" your parents?

4. What happens to the marriage relationship when it doesn't receive enough attention and other things become a higher priority?

Training Principle #2: Build Oneness

The Genesis 2 passage also mentions that a husband and wife "shall become one flesh." Besides the obvious sexual meaning, this indicates that a man and wife also become one emotionally and spiritually. Oneness in marriage is the total uniting of two lives.

5. In what ways have you and your spouse experienced oneness during the time you have been married?

Training Principle #3:
Make a Lifelong Commitment

Read Matthew 19:3–6.

> And Pharisees came up to him and tested him by ask-
> ing, "Is it lawful to divorce one's wife for any cause?"
> He answered, "Have you not read that he who created
> them from the beginning made them male and fe-
> male, and said, 'Therefore a man shall leave his father
> and his mother and hold fast to his wife, and they
> shall become one flesh'? So they are no longer two but
> one flesh. What therefore God has joined together, let
> not man separate."

6. In this passage Jesus says no one should separate what God
   has joined together. Why do you think God places such
   importance on the covenant of marriage?

7. Lifelong commitment is becoming increasingly rare in our
   culture. How does it help a marriage when both husband
   and wife are totally committed to staying together for a
   lifetime?

homebuilders principle: With the challenges that accompany a military marriage, a couple must decide to make a radical commitment to each other.

We all face different challenges in marriage, but in every situation we have a choice. We can either allow the challenge to draw us closer to each other, or to push us apart. These are choices between oneness and isolation.

In the remainder of this study we will look at some of the unique issues faced in the military and how we can make choices that build oneness in marriage. One of these common challenges is the Permanent Change of Station (PCS).

A PCS in Bible Times

In Genesis 12:1–5, we find the story of Abram and Sarai.

> Now the LORD said to Abram, "Go from your country and your kindred and your father's house to the land that I will show you. And I will make of you a great nation, and I will bless you and make your name great, so that you will be a blessing. I will bless those who bless you, and him who dishonors you I will curse, and in you all the families of the earth shall be blessed."
>
> So Abram went, as the LORD had told him, and Lot went with him. Abram was seventy-five years old when he departed from Haran. And Abram took Sarai

his wife, and Lot his brother's son, and all their pos-
sessions that they had gathered, and the people that
they had acquired in Haran, and they set out to go to
the land of Canaan.

8. In what ways is the experience of Abram and Sarai simi-
lar to the sacrifices a military couple will make because
of changing assignments? What range of emotions do you
face as you prepare for a move?

9. Earlier we talked about three basic training principles for
your marriage:

- Make your marriage a priority.
- Build oneness.
- Make a lifelong commitment.

Why are these commitments so crucial to the success of
the marriage relationship when couples make a PCS?

make a date

Set a time for you and your spouse to complete the HomeBuilders project together before the next group meeting. You will be asked at the next session to share an insight or experience from the project.

date _____ time _____

location _____

homebuilders project

On Your Own

1. What do you think causes couples to begin drifting apart in their relationship?

2. What pressures do you currently face that, if not addressed, could push you toward isolation in your marriage?

3. Military couples often face stressful situations due to frequent moves and separations caused by required training

or deployment. Therefore, they need to make a conscious decision to recommit themselves to one another and to their marriage.

What does the word *vow* mean to you?

4. When you joined the military, you took a vow that started like this: "I do solemnly swear (or affirm) that I will support and defend the Constitution of the United States against all enemies, foreign and domestic; that I will bear true faith and allegiance to the same . . . "

What would happen to you if you broke this vow in some way?

5. Below is a typical set of marriage vows:

> **GROOM:** I take this woman to be my lawfully wedded wife. I solemnly promise, before God and these witnesses, that I will love, honor, and cherish her; and that, forsaking all others for her alone, I will perform unto her all the duties that a husband owes to his wife, until God, by death, shall separate us.
> **BRIDE:** I take this man to be my lawfully wedded husband. I solemnly promise, before God and these

witnesses, that I will love, honor, and cherish him,
and that, forsaking all others for him alone, I will per-
form unto him all the duties that a wife owes to her
husband, until God, by death, shall separate us.

What similarities do you see between the vow of allegiance
taken when someone joins the military and the vow taken
when joining in holy matrimony before God?

6. Read Deuteronomy 23:21–23. How do you think God views
a vow taken before Him?

7. In what ways can you work to keep the vows you ex-
changed in your wedding ceremony?

With Your Spouse

1. Share your responses to the questions you answered on
your own.

2. Read the wedding vows out loud to each other.

3. Agree on two things you will do as a couple during the
next week to build oneness in your relationship.

2

Communicating in
the Trenches

Meet each other's needs for communication, even
during separations due to deployment.

warm-up

1. Share how many separations due to military deployments
   or training you have experienced since you have been
   married. Then offer one piece of advice for dealing with
   separations that you have found helpful in your marriage.

2. In three minutes or less, tell about one funny thing that
   has happened to you individually or as a family during a
   deployment or move.

Separation Blues

Married couples often say that their greatest challenges are in the area of communication. Life in the military can place some unusual pressure on this crucial part of a relationship.

Case Study

Betty thought, *If I have to drag these bags out from under the bed one more time so Steve can deploy, I think I'll scream.* It seemed like just yesterday they had talked about joining the military as an interim job until something else came along. And now they were at ten years, six moves, and too many separations to count.

She was surprised to find that she really didn't mind moving so many times. She actually enjoyed seeing new parts of the world and making so many wonderful friends. She was glad their children had a greater understanding of different cultures. She didn't even mind some of the times that Steve had to travel. At first they would act like newlyweds each time he would return. But the honeymoon of those reunions ended all too quickly.

Over the last few years the separations came more frequently, and they felt like a greater ordeal than they had in the past. Between keeping up with household responsibilities and caring for three active children between the ages of six and ten, she felt a huge weight of responsibility. And then when Steve returned, just when she desperately needed relief, he always seemed to need a few days to readjust to home life and to become involved with the kids again.

On top of that, Betty longed to share with Steve her fears about his recent deployments to dangerous places. She desperately wanted to tell him how worried she was over the friends their children were choosing. She knew they needed to talk more about their finances and their future. In fact, they needed to discuss a lot of things, but they seemed to talk less and less these days. And now, with Steve about to leave again, the last thing she wanted to do was rock the boat. After all, what if some of these things made him more anxious while he was gone? So, once again, she would say nothing . . . perhaps when he got home from this trip they would take time to talk.

Steve was in the other room working through some last-minute details before heading out the door. He, too, was lost in thought about his upcoming deployment. He wasn't worried about the trip as much as he was concerned about leaving Betty. In the past she had supported his decision to stay in the military, and even encouraged him to put in for advanced training. But lately, she seemed withdrawn and hard to understand.

He wondered if she was beginning to resent all their moves through the years. She always kept up a brave face, but it must hurt to pull up their roots so often.

All he wanted was to take care of his family. He wanted to leave knowing that Betty and the kids were safe, and that they would be here when he returned. He didn't want to have to think about things at home going wrong while he was away.

He was confident that Betty was perfectly capable of handling just about any situation. After all, hadn't she made all the arrangements for their last move while he had gone ahead of the family to his new job? Wasn't she the one who had caused them all to laugh when they discovered that the movers had packed their week-old garbage in their shipment that was heading overseas?

He just didn't want Betty to become too accustomed to his absences. If she did, she might decide she could actually handle things fine without him. Well, he would think about that later. Right now he needed to focus on getting ready to leave.

1. What do you think might happen to Steve and Betty if they don't resolve their communication breakdown?

2. Which of the issues that Steve and Betty faced could you relate to individually and as a couple?

3. Why do you think military couples are often hesitant to talk about their concerns before and after separations?

4. If both spouses are on active duty, what additional issues might they experience?

Meeting Your Spouse's Needs

We do not have time in one session to discuss all Scripture says about communication in marriage, but we can focus on some biblical principles that will help you deal with the issues military couples face due to frequent or lengthy separations.

5. List some of the common themes you find in the following scriptures.

So if there is any encouragement in Christ, any comfort from love, any participation in the Spirit, any affection and sympathy, complete my joy by being of the same mind, having the same love, being in full accord and of one mind. Do nothing from rivalry or conceit, but in humility count others more significant than yourselves. Let each of you look not only to his own interests, but also to the interests of others. (Philippians 2:1–4)

Finally, all of you, have unity of mind, sympathy, brotherly love, a tender heart, and a humble mind. (1 Peter 3:8)

Let no corrupting talk come out of your mouths, but only such as is good for building up, as fits the occasion, that it may give grace to those who hear. (Ephesians 4:29)

6. Think of some practical ways a married couple could apply these scriptures:

   - before a separation

   - during a separation

   - after a separation

7. Philippians 2:4 instructs us to look "not only to [our] own interests, but also to the interests of others." If you were to apply this to your marriage, how might it change the way you look at communicating with your spouse?

Making It Practical

Answer the next two questions with your spouse.

8. Looking back to the case study, what could Steve and Betty do to address their communication problems?

9. Once a couple recognizes the need for honest, open communication when preparing for a separation, how can they maintain that level of communication during deployment?

homebuilders principle: To build a strong marriage in the midst of the pressures of a military lifestyle, couples must make a commitment to meeting each other's needs through continual, open communication.

make a date

Set a time for you and your spouse to complete the HomeBuilders project together before the next group meeting. You will be asked at the next session to share an insight or experience from the project.

date _____ time _____

location _____

homebuilders project

On Your Own

1. Make a list of five or more emotional issues that seem to recur as you and your spouse prepare for separations. (For example, fear, fatigue from single parenting, loneliness, not being available when needed, and so on.)

2. After making your list, circle the two issues that you struggle with the most. Pray for godly wisdom to know how to communicate these struggles to your spouse.

3. How do you think your list may differ from the list your spouse creates? What issue do you think he or she struggles with the most?

4. Many couples have found different ways to stay connected while apart. The following list highlights some ways to combat isolation. In the column that applies to you, put an X in the boxes to indicate the methods you will use to stay in touch with your spouse. Indicate the frequency with which you plan or desire to implement that method.

Method	Deployed Spouse	Spouse at Home	Frequency
Phone calls			
E-mails			
Texts			
Skype			
Letters			
Letters left with friends			
Work through a devotional study together			
Cards left with friends to be delivered on key dates			
Arrange for flowers or small gifts			
Put notes inside luggage or hide them at home			
Keep pictures so you and others can see them			

With Your Spouse

1. Share your responses to questions 1–3 that you answered on your own. Be open and understanding as you discuss these issues.

2. Now that you understand some of the issues your spouse struggles with, what can you do to help meet some of his or her needs before, during, and after a deployment?

3. After completing this project, how do you better understand the effect the military's mobile lifestyle has on your spouse?

4. Together, look at the charts you completed on your own (question 4). Discuss plans for staying connected during your next separation.

3

More-Month-than-
Money Blues

Prioritize financial needs and work through
challenges unique to career military families.

warm-up

Newlywed Game

Instruct the husbands to leave the room, and then have the wives answer the following questions on paper. Bring the husbands back and see if they can guess how their wives answered the questions.

1. If you went on a remote assignment for one year and could only take one personal item with you—item, not person—what would you take and why?
2. What do you think your spouse would take?
3. Name one special thing you would buy for your spouse if the cost were not an issue.
4. What would your spouse buy for you?

blueprints

Finances and Isolation

While it's impossible to avoid conflict in marriage—it's inevitable even in the best of relationships—it is possible to learn how to work through it. One key is to address the source of conflict. Many couples report that financial decisions and pressures spark more conflict than any other issue.

1. From what you've observed, what are some of the typical challenges military couples have with money, especially during their first years in the service?

2. In what ways do financial struggles cause a couple to experience increased isolation from each other?

homebuilders principle: To build oneness in marriage, military couples need to work together to manage their finances.

Scriptural Principles on Handling Money

3. If someone were to examine your checking account and credit card records, what conclusions would he reach about your financial priorities—the most important things to which you allocate money?

4. The Bible includes more than two thousand verses dealing with money and money management. What do the following passages tell us about what our financial priorities should be?

For the same reason you also pay taxes, for the authorities are ministers of God, attending to this very thing. Pay to all what is owed to them: taxes to whom taxes are owed, revenue to whom revenue is owed, respect to whom respect is owed, honor to whom honor is owed. Owe no one anything, except to love each other, for the one who loves another has fulfilled the law. (Romans 13:6–8)

But if anyone does not provide for his relatives, and especially for members of his household, he has denied the faith and is worse than an unbeliever. (1 Timothy 5:8)

Honor the LORD with your wealth and with the first-fruits of all your produce. (Proverbs 3:9)

Go to the ant, O sluggard; consider her ways, and be wise. Without having any chief, officer, or ruler, she prepares her bread in summer and gathers her food in harvest. How long will you lie there, O sluggard? When will you arise from your sleep? A little sleep, a little slumber, a little folding of the hands to rest, and poverty will come upon you like a robber, and want like an armed man. (Proverbs 6:6–11)

5. Borrowing money usually prevents couples from achieving long-term financial success. What reasons do people often give for borrowing money (whether from another person, a lending institution, or a credit card)? Which of these do you think are legitimate reasons for borrowing money?

6. What do the following verses have to say about borrowing money?

> The wicked borrows but does not pay back, but the righteous is generous and gives. (Psalm 37:21)

> The rich rules over the poor, and the borrower is the slave of the lender. (Proverbs 22:7)

7. What suggestions would you give for staying out of debt?

8. What have you learned by watching how other couples handle their finances while coping with deployments and moves?

homebuilders principle: Military couples can trust that God will provide for their needs and then learn to live within His provision.

9. Answer this question with your spouse: What do you think we need to do to begin ordering our finances around biblical priorities?

10. If appropriate, share with the group something you and your spouse discussed in the previous question.

make a date

Set a time for you and your spouse to complete the HomeBuilders project together before the next group meeting. You will be asked at the next session to share an insight or experience from the project.

date _____ time _____

location _____

homebuilders project

On Your Own

1. List the financial areas you think you and your spouse manage well together.

2. List your greatest concerns regarding your personal financial situation.

3. What are your financial goals? What would you like your financial situation to be in one year? Five years? Ten years?

4. What first step can you take to accomplish the one-year goal?

With Your Spouse

1. Share your responses to the questions you answered on your own.

2. What changes do you need to make in how you manage your finances together so you can avoid isolation in this area?

3. List one financial decision you are making right now. Share with each other how you would like to manage this.

4. Before deployment, a military couple should put some important financial and legal documents in a safe place for easy access for the spouse who is at home. Check the following inventory, and make plans to get these documents in place and current.

   • A will. Only 50 percent of all Americans have wills, and most of those are outdated if they have not been reviewed within the past three years.
   • A living trust/will. The legal assistance office can help you make sure your will meets legal standards.

- A record of emergency data, including information about life, health, and car insurance
- A power of attorney document

5. Decide as a couple who will pay the bills and how decisions will be made for larger purchases during deployments or temporary duty.

6. Set a time within the next week to work together on a family budget if you don't already have one in place.

7. Close your time in prayer, asking God to give you the wisdom and discipline to handle your finances well.

4 SEAL Training:
SExual Accountability and Love

Recognize the temptations that can threaten your marriage and take positive steps to keep your covenant.

warm-up

1. Share a funny memory from your wedding or honeymoon. (Remember, don't embarrass your spouse!)
2. What is your idea of the perfect date with your spouse?

blueprints

Case Study: Common Temptations

George lay next to Judy in bed. His long deployment was over. He wasn't sure when he would be traveling again, but for now it was just good to be home. The kids had hung a banner across the front door, saying "Welcome Home, Daddy," along with some balloons. Then a wrestling match of hugs ensued!

After the kids had finally gone to bed, he and Judy had stayed up for hours, talking over things they hadn't discussed in months. When they had finally caught up with how the children were doing, how his trip had been, and how Judy had handled their separation, they experienced an intimacy with each other that he had longed for during their time apart.

He wondered if Judy experienced the same temptations he faced while he was away. It was so hard to be away from his wife for several months. He was proud that he had never cheated on her, but it wasn't easy. During his time overseas he had ample opportunity to read explicit magazines, be drawn to online porn, watch movies he'd never want his wife to see, and fantasize about being with other women. Sometimes, in his loneliness, he struck up conversations with women, and on one occasion he had to pull back because he could see that the relationship might become too personal.

Each time he came home to his wife and family, he experienced a level of love he knew could never be replaced by those other fantasies. But why couldn't he remember that while he was away? What could he do differently to protect his marriage the next time he was gone from home?

Judy smiled and, half asleep, thought about their reunion. It was so good to have George home. She could relax now and let him handle some of the issues that had arisen while he was away. However, she knew he couldn't help her handle everything that had gone on while he had been deployed.

She had been so determined not to put herself in a situation that would compromise their marriage. She didn't flirt, and only went out for evenings with friends if she was certain the setting would be safe and neutral. So she was surprised when her temptation came from an unlikely source—a man she had worked with for years. They were working on a project together, and their work often spilled over into long lunches. She enjoyed their conversation; it made her feel attractive to have another man show interest in her.

As the weeks passed during George's absence, she found herself thinking more and more about this man. She realized she didn't know him that well, but she couldn't help comparing him to George. She fantasized about spending more time with him, perhaps on a real date.

Now that George was home, those thoughts seemed hollow and foolish. *I'll do better next time George is gone*, she promised herself.

1. In what ways were George and Judy putting their relationship in jeopardy during his deployment?

2. What advice would you give each of them about how to protect the sanctity of their marriage?

3. Do you think it is possible to eliminate temptation from your life? If not, how do you think you could reduce temptation in your life?

Protecting Your Marriage

4. What promise do you find in 1 Corinthians 10:13? How could you apply this to your life and marriage? What is an example of a "way of escape"?

> No temptation has overtaken you that is not common to man. God is faithful, and he will not let you be tempted beyond your ability, but with the temptation he will also provide the way of escape, that you may be able to endure it. (1 Corinthians 10:13)

As we look at additional scriptures about temptation, it becomes clear that we need to take both defensive and offensive actions to protect ourselves from temptation and maintain fidelity in marriage.

5. Read Proverbs 5:18–23.

> Let your fountain be blessed, and rejoice in the wife
> of your youth, a lovely deer, a graceful doe. Let her
> breasts fill you at all times with delight; be intoxicated
> always in her love. Why should you be intoxicated, my
> son, with a forbidden woman and embrace the bosom
> of an adulteress? For a man's ways are before the eyes
> of the LORD, and he ponders all his paths. The iniqui-
> ties of the wicked ensnare him, and he is held fast in
> the cords of his sin. He dies for lack of discipline, and
> because of his great folly he is led astray.

- Defense: According to this passage, what should motivate
  us to flee temptation (vv. 21–23)?

- Offense: One of the best things you can do is to be exhila-
  rated by the love of your spouse. For many of us, this means
  rekindling the sparks of romance that can easily begin
  to cool during years of marriage. Turn to your spouse to
  answer the following question: What are some of the most
  romantic things we've done to build love in our marriage?
  Then share one or two of your answers with the group.

6. Read 2 Timothy 2:22.

> So flee youthful passions and pursue righteousness,
> faith, love, and peace, along with those who call on
> the Lord from a pure heart.

- Defense: What do you think it means to "flee youthful passions"? How can you apply this principle to some of the temptations you commonly face?

- Offense: What does it mean to "pursue righteousness, faith, love, and peace, along with those who call on the Lord from a pure heart"? How can you apply this to your life?

Accountability

Read the following scriptures.

> Bear one another's burdens, and so fulfill the law of Christ. (Galatians 6:2)

> Let the word of Christ dwell in you richly, teaching and admonishing one another in all wisdom, singing psalms and hymns and spiritual songs, with thankfulness in your hearts to God. (Colossians 3:16)

> But exhort one another every day, as long as it is called "today," that none of you may be hardened by the deceitfulness of sin. (Hebrews 3:13)

Therefore, confess your sins to one another and pray
for one another, that you may be healed. The prayer
of a righteous person has great power as it is working.
(James 5:16)

7. How do the ways of relating with other Christians, as
described in these scriptures, also help protect and enrich
your marriage?

8. In Ephesians 5:21 we are told to "[submit] to one another
out of reverence for Christ." This is the principle of accountability—submitting your life, in the spirit of the
scriptures we just examined, to the scrutiny of another
person. Accountability means asking another person for
advice and spiritual counsel, and giving him or her the
freedom to make honest observations and evaluations
about you.

During deployment or separations an individual should try
to establish accountability with others he or she can trust (never
have accountability with a member of the opposite sex). Accountability partners should be able to openly discuss their struggles
and temptations. They should be able to ask some difficult questions and then pray for each other.

The following questions can be helpful in an accountability relationship:

- Have you struggled with temptation recently? If so, what was the temptation? Be specific.

- Have you been in contact with your spouse while you have been separated? What have you done to keep the lines of communication open? Are you still captivated by his or her love? Can you be more diligent in this area?

- Are you being completely honest with me in all of your answers?

Building a Wall of Protection

9. Turn to your spouse to answer the following: What one idea have we discussed in this session that we can apply in order to build a protective wall around our marriage?

🏠 **homebuilders principle:** We can preserve the sanctity of our marriage by dealing with temptation and by remaining sexually faithful.

10. As you come to the end of this study, reflect as a group on what you have experienced. Pick one of the following questions to answer and share with the group.

- What has this group meant to you during the course of this study? Be specific.
- What is the most valuable thing you discovered?
- How have you changed as a result of what you've learned in this study?
- What would you like to see happen next for this group?

make a date

Set a time for you and your spouse to complete the HomeBuilders project together before the next group meeting. You will be asked at the next session to share an insight or experience from the project.

date _____ time _____

location _____

homebuilders project

On Your Own

1. Review the scriptures we examined during the group session, ending with 1 Corinthians 10:13. Ask God to reveal any areas where you have been dealing with temptation. If necessary, ask for His forgiveness.

   Thank Him for forgiving you and loving you. Pray that He would give you the strength to protect yourself from future temptations.

2. Make a list of other men (if you are the husband) or women (if you are the wife) whom you can ask to become your accountability partners while you and your spouse are separated due to an assignment. This would generally be one or two other people; you would meet with them, discuss areas in which you know you are weak, and agree to honestly answer questions they will ask you. (For example, someone who has trouble avoiding movies with sexual content would have his accountability partner ask specifically if he watched any of these movies during the separation.)

3. Men and women have different emotional and physical needs. What are your physical needs just prior to a deployment? What are your emotional needs? What do you think your spouse's needs are?

4. Sometimes the reunion after a deployment can be just as stressful as the time leading up to departure. A husband's and wife's needs vary when they are first reunited as a couple and as a family. Compare how your emotional and physical needs are different after a reunion to what they are just prior to the separation. How do you think your spouse's needs differ?

With Your Spouse

1. Share your responses to the questions you answered on your own.

2. Affirm your spouse on how he or she meets your emotional and physical needs. In an open and loving manner, share other needs you have that you haven't yet discussed.

3. Decide on two things you can do as individuals or as a couple to protect your marriage.

4. Close your time in prayer, thanking God for the experience you've had with the HomeBuilders group and for how He has worked in your marriage.

where do you go from here?

Couples around the world are discovering their own ministry by becoming a Military HomeBuilder. For more information, visit MilitaryMinistry.org. Also, consider some of these next steps:

Small Group

- Commit to continue building marriages by doing another small-group study such as *Making Your Marriage Deployment Ready* or for parents, *Defending the Military Family*. Challenge others in your church or chapel to form Home-Builders groups focused on the military.
- Consider the other HomeBuilders studies. They all benefit military marriages.

Retreat

- Attend a FamilyLife Weekend to Remember®. (Many of these have a military emphasis.) Invite military couples from your small group and church or chapel to attend with you.
- Use FamilyLife's The Art of Marriage® to encourage your military couples in God's designs for marriage.
- Military Ministry has additional ideas for how you can use HomeBuilder material in a retreat setting. Visit Military Ministry.org, or call 1-800-444-6006 for details.

Men and Women

- Offer a men's Stepping Up® video event or small-group study. For more information, visit MenSteppingUp.com. This material is excellent for men who want to grow as leaders in their homes, churches, and communities. It also contains many military illustrations.
- Offer a small-group Bible study for women using *Loving Your Military Man*. Based on Philippians 4:8, this is a ten-week study that will encourage military wives to grow in their relationship with their husbands and with God.

our problems, God's answers

Every couple has to deal with problems in marriage—communication problems, money problems, difficulties with sexual intimacy, and more. Learning how to handle these issues is important to cultivating a strong and loving relationship.

The Big Problem

One basic problem is at the heart of every other problem in marriage, and it's too big for any person to deal with on his or her own. The problem is separation from God. If you want to experience life and marriage the way they were designed to be, you need a vital relationship with the God who created you.

But sin separates us from God. Some try to deal with sin by working hard to become better people. They may read books on how to control anger, or they may resolve to stop cheating on their taxes, but in their hearts they know—we all know—that the sin problem runs much deeper than bad habits and will take more than our best behavior to overcome it. In reality, we have rebelled against God. We have ignored Him and have decided to run our lives in a way that makes sense to us, thinking that our ideas and plans are better than His.

> For all have sinned and fall short of the glory of God.
> (Romans 3:23)

What does it mean to "fall short of the glory of God"? It means that none of us has trusted and treasured God the way we should. We have sought to satisfy ourselves with other things and have treated them as more valuable than God. We have gone our own way. According to the Bible, we have to pay a penalty for our sin. We cannot simply do things the way we choose and hope it will be okay with God. Following our own plans leads to our destruction.

> There is a way that seems right to a man, but its end is
> the way to death. (Proverbs 14:12)

> For the wages of sin is death. (Romans 6:23)

The penalty for sin is that we are separated from God's love. God is holy, and we are sinful. No matter how hard we try, we cannot come up with some plan, like living a good life or even trying to do what the Bible says, and hope that we can avoid the penalty.

God's Solution to Sin

Thankfully, God has a way to solve our dilemma. He became a man through the person of Jesus Christ. Jesus lived a holy life in perfect obedience to God's plan. He also willingly died on a cross to pay our penalty for sin. Then He proved that He is more powerful than sin or death by rising from the dead. He alone has the power to pay the penalty for our sin.

> Jesus said to him, "I am the way, and the truth, and
> the life. No one comes to the Father except through me."
> (John 14:6)

> But God shows his love for us in that while we were
> still sinners, Christ died for us. (Romans 5:8)

> For the wages of sin is death, but the free gift
> of God is eternal life in Christ Jesus our Lord.
> (Romans 6:23)

The death and resurrection of Jesus have fixed our sin problem. He has bridged the gap between God and us. He is calling us to come to Him and to give up our flawed plans for running our lives. He wants us to trust God and His plan.

Accepting God's Solution

If you recognize that you are separated from God, He is calling you to confess your sins. All of us have made messes of our lives because we have stubbornly preferred our ideas and plans to His. As a result, we deserve to be cut off from God's love and His care for us. But God has promised that if we will acknowledge that we have rebelled against His plan, He will forgive us and will fix our sin problem.

> But to all who did receive him, who believed in his
> name, he gave the right to become children of God.
> (John 1:12)

> For by grace you have been saved through faith.
> And this is not your own doing; it is the gift of God,
> not a result of works, so that no one may boast.
> (Ephesians 2:8–9)

When the Bible talks about receiving Christ, it means we acknowledge that we are sinners and that we can't fix the problem ourselves. It means we turn away from our sin. And it means we trust Christ to forgive our sins and to make us the kind of people He wants us to be. It's not enough to intellectually believe that Christ is the Son of God. We must trust in Him and His plan for our lives by faith, as an act of the will.

Are things right between you and God, with Him and His plan at the center of your life? Or is life spinning out of control as you seek to make your own way?

If you have been trying to make your own way, you can decide today to change. You can turn to Christ and allow Him to transform your life. All you need to do is talk to Him and tell Him what is stirring in your mind and in your heart. If you've never done this, consider taking the steps listed here:

- Do you agree that you need God? Tell God.
- Have you made a mess of your life by following your own plan? Tell God.
- Do you want God to forgive you? Tell God.
- Do you believe that Jesus' death on the cross and His resurrection from the dead gave Him the power to fix your sin problem and to grant you the free gift of eternal life? Tell God.
- Are you ready to acknowledge that God's plan for your life is better than any plan you could come up with? Tell God.
- Do you agree that God has the right to be the Lord and Master of your life? Tell God.

"Seek the LORD while he may be found; call upon him while he is near." (Isaiah 55:6)

Here is a suggested prayer:

Lord Jesus, I need you. Thank You for dying on the cross for my sins. I receive You as my Savior and Lord. Thank You for forgiving my sins and giving me eternal life. Make me the kind of person You want me to be.

The Christian Life

For the person who is a follower of Christ—a Christian—the penalty for sin is paid in full. But the effect of sin continues throughout our lives.

If we say we have no sin, we deceive ourselves, and the truth is not in us. (1 John 1:8)

For I do not do the good I want, but the evil I do not want is what I keep on doing. (Romans 7:19)

The effects of sin carry over into our marriages as well. Even Christians struggle to maintain solid, God-honoring marriages. Most couples eventually realize they can't do it on their own. But with God's help, they can succeed. To learn more, read the extended version of this article at FamilyLife.com/Resources.

leader's notes

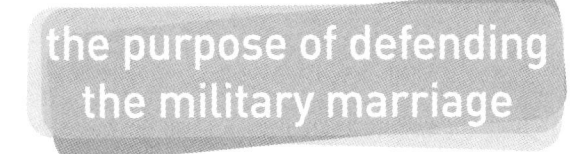

the purpose of defending the military marriage

This study is designed to give military couples a tool to help them cope with some of the unique stresses and challenges they face in their marriages. By participating in this study, couples will strengthen their relationships and learn practical steps they can take to make their marriages more solid.

The intended audience of this study would be active duty, reserve, and National Guard military members and their spouses. We also recognize that others who work with and for the military—DOD teachers or civilian employees, for example—would also benefit from the study.

Most people today enter into marriage with little idea of how to make the relationship work. If they happen to be in the military, they routinely face challenges that put an incredible strain on their relationship, such as

- extended separations from spouses and families,
- long duty hours,
- fear for loved ones who may be in dangerous situations,
- moving frequently to unfamiliar environments, and
- overseas assignments.

Leader qualifications

Leading a HomeBuilders group does not require an expert Bible teacher or a couple with a "perfect" marriage. The leader of the group is a facilitator, not a lecturer. The main function of the facilitator is to provide an environment of openness, warmth, and acceptance.

The facilitator is a fellow member of the group who has the added responsibility of guiding the group in the right direction within the set time period (sixty minutes). The best leaders are couples willing to share their successes and weaknesses while trying to foster a better marriage at the same time.

If you are unsure about your ability to lead, consider coleading with another couple. You can divide the responsibilities. Together you can trust God to work in your lives and to help other couples.

Starting a HomeBuilders group

As a couple, commit to each other and to God to make the Home-Builders group a priority for the time it will take to complete the study. (Remember, it only requires a short-term commitment. You may choose to meet weekly or every other week.) Decide how you will share responsibility for organizing and leading the group, preparing for the session, making phone calls, and details of hospitality.

Inviting couples to participate

You may want to ask your chaplain if he knows of any couples who would be interested and if you could promote the group within the chapel (see below). Invite friends, neighbors, coworkers, and parents from your children's school or teams. A personal invitation is always best.

This study also can be used in Gateway Ministries as young men and women prepare for military duty. It would be appropriate for senior cadets at academies as they look toward their first assignment and possibly marriage. Engaged couples living in the United States or overseas who are considering joining the military would also benefit.

We should mention that the content is designed primarily for couples who do not know much about the Bible. Couples who are already mature in their Christian faith may find the content very basic; we advise them to see the group as an opportunity to reach out and help couples who are younger in the faith.

Show potential group members the materials and tell them about the discussion format. You will want to assure couples that the study will help make a good marriage better, and that they will be making a limited time commitment.

An ideal size for the group is four to seven couples (including you and your spouse).

Starting HomeBuilders in your chapel

If you are interested in starting HomeBuilders in your chapel, volunteer to lead a group there. Make it clear to your chaplain that you will do the work, and show him or her the HomeBuilders material.

Explain how the principles from the study have affected your life, and share how chapels can use HomeBuilders in a variety of ways. But if the chaplain is not interested, respect his or her wishes and start a neighborhood group instead.

Small groups

Chapels most frequently use HomeBuilders studies in small groups or as an evening Bible study. If small groups already exist at your chapel, talk with the person who makes decisions on the curriculum. If there are no small groups currently meeting, you could offer to organize the first group.

Retreats or weekend emphasis

A chapel or Sunday school class often sets aside a weekend to emphasize strong marriages. This provides a great setting to share a series of HomeBuilders sessions.

Sunday school

There are two important adaptations that will need to be made if you want to use this study in a classroom setting:

1. The material you cover will need to focus on the content from the Blueprints section of each session. Blueprints is the heart of each session and is designed to last approximately forty-five minutes.
2. Most Sunday school classes are geared around a teaching format instead of a small-group format. If this study is to be used in a class setting, the class will need to adapt to a small-group dynamic. This will involve an interactive, discussion-based format, and may also require a class to break into multiple smaller groups. (We recommend groups of six to eight people.)

Promotion Ideas

- Advertise in base newspapers, at Family Support centers, and through command channels.
- Send invitations to chapel members and neighbors.
- Advertise in the chapel bulletin, newsletter, or flyers.
- Conduct an introductory meeting to demonstrate the effectiveness and fun of HomeBuilders.
- Have your chaplain endorse HomeBuilders from the pulpit.
- Use sign-up sheets.
- Invite your chaplain or Sunday school teacher to observe an existing class.

Child care

It is important that your group focus on the study material without distractions and interruptions. Ask your group what works best for them. Child care must be dependable. Some couples will not be able to commit to every group session if child care is not provided. Here are some suggestions:

- Arrange babysitting in one house and hold the study in another.
- Pool resources to hire a babysitter.
- Ask if any couples have older children who would babysit.
- Use available child care or chapel facilities when the nursery is already scheduled to be open.
- Hold your group meetings at the same time as chapel Awana or other children's programs.

Leading a HomeBuilders group

Before you begin each session, agree as a couple how much you will communicate about your own marriage. Sharing openly will help others apply biblical truths to their own lives. Study the leader's notes and pray regularly for your group.

Also, discuss as a couple your leadership responsibilities for each session. It is also important to practice hospitality. Making friends is a key to creating an environment in which God will change lives.

In our impersonal world, many couples are hungry for friendships. God will use your relationships in an atmosphere of mild accountability to encourage couples to apply the lessons to their lives.

Starting the session

Share the following ground rules at the beginning of the first session, and review them as needed:

- Share nothing that will embarrass your spouse.
- You may pass on any question.
- Anything shared in the group stays in the group.
- Couples should complete the HomeBuilders project between each session.

Simply read through the questions to lead the study. At first, you may need to wait for answers. Don't jump in too quickly with your own ideas. Naturally, couples will wait for you to answer, and by doing so, you will end up teaching the material without their input. Ideas you can solicit from the group will mean more to the participants than those you teach. When discussion lasts too long or gets off the subject, just read the next question to stay on track.

Components of each session

Warm-Up (5–10 minutes)
The purpose of Warm-Up is to help people unwind from a busy day and get to know each other better. The questions also lead them toward the topic of that session.

Blueprints (45 minutes)
This is the heart of the study. In this time, people answer pertinent questions related to the topic of study and look to God's Word for understanding.

HomeBuilders Project (60 minutes)
This is the unique application step in a HomeBuilders study. Before your meeting ends, couples are encouraged to Make a Date to complete this project with their spouse before the next meeting. Encourage couples to make this a priority—it will make the HomeBuilders experience twice as effective.

Additional tips

1. Keep the focus on what Scripture says. When someone disagrees with Scripture, affirm him for wrestling with the issue and point out that some biblical statements are hard to

understand or accept. Encourage him to keep an open mind on the issue at least through the remainder of the sessions.

2. Avoid labeling an answer as "wrong"; doing so can kill the atmosphere for discussion. Encourage a person who gives a wrong or incomplete answer to look again at the question or the scripture being explored. Offer a comment such as, "That's really close" or "There's something else we need to see there." Or ask others in the group to respond.

3. Your best resource for communicating with others is your own life and marriage. Be prepared to get the discussion going by sharing things from your own lives. But as a couple, be sure you agree beforehand about the issues and experiences you will share.

4. One thing to watch is the possibility of people in the group using the discussion as an opportunity to focus too much on their perceived shortcomings of the military. Though many questions call for couples to discuss the pressures they face in marriage because of the military lifestyle, encourage them to avoid getting sidetracked into "military bashing."

5. Take time during each session to encourage couples to work on the HomeBuilders project before you meet again. These projects are a vital part of the HomeBuilders experience.

Praying in the group

An important part of a small group is prayer. However, as the leader you need to be sensitive to the level of comfort the people in your group have toward praying in front of others.

Never call on people to pray aloud if you don't know if they are comfortable doing this. There are a number of creative approaches you can take, such as modeling prayer yourself, calling for volunteers, and letting people state their prayers in the form of finishing a sentence. A tool that is helpful in a group is a prayer list. You should lead the prayer time, but allow another couple in the group the opportunity to create, update, and distribute prayer lists as a ministry to the group.

Refreshments

Many groups choose to have refreshments because they help create an environment of fellowship. Here are a couple of suggestions:

- For the first session you should provide the refreshments and then allow the group to be involved by having a sign-up sheet.
- Consider starting your group with a short time of informal fellowship and refreshments (fifteen minutes), then move into the study. This way if a couple is late, they only miss the food and don't disrupt the study.

Building new leadership

As you lead, look for potential leaders who might multiply your group into new groups. Someone may even express interest in leading. Here are a few pointers to help you build new leaders:

- Look for others who demonstrate availability, teachability, and faithfulness.

- Select a couple in your group who demonstrates maturity in their Christian walk and marriage, and whom you feel would be good discussion leaders.
- Invite them to try out the leadership role by asking one or two questions, by leading part of the session, and then leading an entire session by the end of the study.
- Challenge them to start a group after the current study is completed.

Blueprints commentary

In the Blueprints commentary section are some additional notes about various Blueprints questions and possible answers. The numbers below correspond to the Blueprints question numbers. Notes are not included for every question. Most questions are designed to help you make sure group members understand the correct scriptural principles.

Many of the questions in this study are designed so group members can draw from their own opinions and experiences. If you share any of these points, be sure to do so in a manner that does not stifle discussion by making you the authority with the final answers. Begin your comments by saying things like, "One thing I notice in this passage is ... " or "I think another reason for this is ...."

session one

basic training

***(The numbers below correspond
to the Blueprints question they relate to.)***

1. The military lifestyle offers opportunities for travel and
   adventures that most other families would not have. These
   experiences can build positive memories. Separations,
   although painful, can strengthen a relationship. Shared
   adversity can build a common bond.

2. Separations due to deployments, field exercises, and temporary duty cause strain on any relationship. The need for
   communication increases. Permanent moves (PCS) cause
   strain due to having to say goodbye to old friends, make
   new friends, and learn a new area.

3. Leaving your parents means making your relationship
   with your spouse your top priority. Your marriage relationship should come before your relationship with your
   parents. This means moving dependency for emotional,
   financial, and spiritual support from one's parents to one's
   spouse. For some couples, it is difficult to place the needs
   of a spouse ahead of parents' needs, and for some parents
   it is difficult to let their child go—not just physically, but
   emotionally.

4. Sometimes people allow other relationships—with family or friends—to become more important. Or they allow work and career to be top priority. It's also common to be more committed to entertainment, self-fulfillment, leisure activities, or hobbies. Eventually, these other priorities can cause you to experience isolation from your spouse.

6. Marriage is the first institution God created, and it is a foundation of society. God knows the damage that happens in divorce. It hurts people emotionally, and it destroys families. And when families are destroyed, the culture suffers.

7. This mindset will give couples a different perspective on the inevitable problems, conflicts, and pressures they will face in marriage. They view these as issues to work through rather than issues that may cause them to grow apart.

8. Abram surely felt sadness and grief as he left friends and family behind. He was probably anxious about moving into an unknown future. He may have also felt excited about the adventure ahead. To deal with these emotions, Abram turned to God in prayer, and Sarai trusted in her husband's faith.

9. Commitment is necessary in order to survive the stresses of multiple moves.

session two

communicating in the trenches

1. If Steve and Betty don't resolve their communication problems they can become increasingly isolated, possibly bitter, and eventually emotionally separated. This could lead to vulnerability to affairs and even divorce.

3. Couples don't want to raise an issue that can't be resolved before they go. They feel guilty about rocking the boat, and are caught in the demands of preparing to deploy.

5. These passages talk of living in humility and peace with one another and putting the needs of others ahead of your own. This is critical for a married couple because selfishness can quickly destroy a marriage.

7. You would be thinking of what your spouse needs to talk about, and you would be willing to do it.

session three

1. Typical problems include not having money, little training or discipline in managing money, poor communication about bills and money while deployed, going into debt, and not having a team approach to handling finances. A lack of a team approach leads to big problems during deployment. Here are some follow-up questions you can use to spark further discussion if you wish:

   How can handling two bank accounts cause financial challenges when a couple is separated due to deployment?

   Why do you think many couples report that the week before receiving a paycheck is often marked by stress and conflict?

4. Romans 13:6–8 speaks of our obligation to pay our bills, pay taxes, and stay out of debt. First Timothy 5:8 instructs us to provide for our relatives and family. Proverbs 3:9 tells us to give back to the Lord from what He has provided for us. Proverbs 6:6–11 encourages us to save for future needs.

5. Occasionally, you may need to borrow money to provide food, housing, and transportation for your family. But debt

should be avoided whenever possible. A mortgage and car loan should be paid off in advance when possible.

6. These passages all speak of the dangers of borrowing money. Borrowing money is not forbidden in the Bible, but it is strongly discouraged. The borrower is servant to the lender. Don't get into debt unless you have the means to pay.

8. Couples who succeed financially usually communicate before and during a deployment about what bills are due, how much money is being spent, and how much is being saved. They have a plan on how to manage their money, and they stick with the plan.

session four

SEAL training

1. George was exposing himself to temptation through pornography, and he was not controlling his thoughts. Both he and Judy are opening themselves up to emotional attachments to others, and this leads them to begin comparing their spouse to others.

2. They need to avoid things that tempt them. George could join or start a Bible study and be accountable to some other Christian men. He could maintain good communication with his wife by e-mail, phone calls, or love letters. He could have her picture always in the open.

3. Spend time in Bible study and prayer daily. Memorize and meditate on appropriate Scripture verses. Be accountable to other people of the same sex. Maintain close communication with each other. Don't read or watch tempting material. Avoid compromising situations. Talk in advance with your accountability partner about potential situations. Pray for each other.

4. You are not alone in your temptation. God will always provide a way to escape or to stand up to temptation if you are willing to trust Him. This applies to all temptation in life, including the sexual temptation you may face while apart.

5. Defense: God sees what we do, and we will suffer the consequences of our actions.

6. Defense: Fleeing youthful passions means turning away from any situation that would tempt you. Sometimes this means averting your eyes when you see an image inadvertently—while passing by a magazine newsstand, for example. It also means avoiding books, magazines, movies, television shows, and websites that tempt you to look at suggestive images.

   Offense: Pursuing the good things—righteousness, faith, hope, love, etc.—means filling your mind and your time with things that draw you closer to God. Do this with others who are heading in the same direction you are.

7. Accountability can help us avoid sin. If you are on deployment, for example, knowing that your partner is going to ask, "Did you read any pornography while you were gone?" will motive you to avoid it. Knowing that someone will be asking us questions about our behavior, our attitudes, and our thought life should motivate us to be more diligent in areas we struggle in.

more tools for leaders

Looking for more ways to help people build their marriages and families?

Thank you for your efforts to help people develop their marriages and families using biblical principles. We recognize the influence that one person—or couple—can have on another, and we'd like to help you multiply your ministry.

FamilyLife® is pleased to offer a wide range of resources in various formats. Visit us online at FamilyLife.com, where you will find information about our

- getaways and events, featuring Weekend to Remember® and The Art of Marriage®, offered in cities throughout the United States;
- multimedia resources for small groups, churches, and community networking;
- interactive products for parents, couples, small-group leaders, and one-to-one mentors; and
- assortment of blogs, forums, and other online connections.

who is familylife?

FamilyLife® is a nonprofit, Christian organization focused on the mission of helping every home become a godly home. Believing that family is the foundation of society, FamilyLife works in more than a hundred countries around the world to build healthier marriages and families through marriage getaways and events, small-group curriculum, *FamilyLife Today*® radio broadcasts, Hope for Orphans® orphan care ministry, the Internet, and a wide range of marriage and family resources.

Dennis and Barbara Rainey are cofounders of FamilyLife. Authors of over twenty-five books and hundreds of articles, they are also popular conference speakers and radio hosts. With six grown children and numerous grandchildren, the Raineys love to encourage couples in building godly marriages and families.